Mentally Unemployable

Contents

Introduction

Do you ever feel like you don't fit in with the traditional work environment? Like you have a unique vision and purpose that can't be fulfilled in a typical 9-5 job? If so, you might be mentally unemployable.

Starting a business isn't for the faint of heart. It takes hard work, dedication, and a willingness to take risks. Plus, it can be isolating and lonely, especially when you don't have the same support network as you would in a traditional job. But, if you're committed to your vision and willing to work, it can be a rewarding and fulfilling way of life.

This eBook will dive into mental unemployability and give you insights and tips for starting your own business or pursuing an entrepreneurial path. We'll discuss the mindset and skills required for success and give you practical advice for overcoming common challenges and obstacles.

And hey, we get it. Starting a business isn't always rainbows and sunshine. It's more like a rollercoaster ride with lots of ups and downs. But you can make it through anything with some humour and a touch of grit. So, if you're ready to take the leap and pursue your dreams of entrepreneurship, join us on this journey and discover what it means to be mentally unemployable.

Copyright

ISBN 978-1-4477-8557-6

Chapter One: Introduction to Mental Unemployability

Have you ever felt like you don't belong in the traditional work environment? Do you dream of being your boss and running your own business? If you answered yes to these questions, you might be experiencing a phenomenon known as mental unemployability.

Mental unemployability is a term used to describe individuals who feel unfulfilled and unsatisfied with traditional employment and instead desire to become entrepreneurs. It is a growing trend in today's society, and more people feel unfulfilled by their traditional 9-5 jobs. As a result, people are now seeking alternative career paths. This can include starting their businesses, working as freelancers or consultants, or pursuing creative endeavors.

This mindset is becoming more common today as people realize that the traditional work model may not fit everyone best. Studies show that the number of self-employed or starting their businesses is rising.

Succeeding as a mentally unemployable individual requires having a clear vision and plan for your business or career path. This can include identifying your strengths and weaknesses, developing a business plan or career strategy, and seeking mentorship and guidance from others pursuing similar paths.

It's also essential to cultivate a mindset of resilience and determination. Starting a business or pursuing a non-traditional career path can be challenging. However, overcoming obstacles and achieving success is possible with persistence and a willingness to learn and adapt.

Networking and building relationships with others in your industry or field can also be helpful for mentally unemployable individuals. Connecting with others who share your passion or purpose can provide valuable support, resources, and connections to help you achieve your goals.

The driving force for Mental unemployability

Mental unemployability is not just about a desire for entrepreneurship. Unlike traditional unemployment, mental unemployability is not necessarily a result of economic factors or a lack of job opportunities. It is a mindset and a desire for something different. It can be driven by various factors, including burnout, boredom, a passion for meaningful work, or a more excellent work-life balance.

A driving factor may be the desire for more flexibility and autonomy or a need to pursue a passion or purpose not fulfilled by traditional employment. For example, you may find yourself in a corporate office and feel unfulfilled with a lack of satisfaction. You may feel like just a tiny cog in a big machine and desire more flexibility in your work life, such as the ability to work from home or set your hours. Furthermore, you may have a passion for the environment and want to pursue a career that aligns with that passion but feel limited by your current job.

Another reason for this shift in mindset is that people are no longer satisfied with having a job that pays the bills. Mental unemployability is a mindset that seeks something more than just a paycheck. Technology has made it easier than ever before to start a business. With the internet, anyone can start a business from anywhere in the world, and social media has made it easier to market and promote products and services.

Challenges of Mental Unemployability

The concept of mental unemployability is fraught with difficulties. Starting a business or pursuing a non-traditional career path can be risky and uncertain. It requires a willingness to take on new challenges and step outside one's comfort zone. It can also require significant time, energy, and resources.

Take Lisa, for instance. She has always been an entrepreneur at heart, but she's been stuck in a traditional job for years. She dreams of starting her own business and being her boss, but leaving a stable job and taking on the risks of entrepreneurship is terrifying. She's unsure if she's ready to invest the time, energy, and resources to turn her dream into a reality.

One of the biggest challenges for those experiencing mental unemployability is the lack of support and understanding from others. Many still view entrepreneurship or non-traditional career paths as risky or unconventional and may not provide the necessary support or encouragement.

Another challenge is the fear of failure. Starting a business or pursuing a non-traditional career path can be intimidating, and the fear of failure can be paralyzing. It's important to remember that failure is a natural part of the learning process and that every successful entrepreneur or creative professional has experienced setbacks and challenges.

While mental unemployability may be challenging, there are solutions to these difficulties. In the latter part of this book, we will dive deeper into the specific strategies for starting a business or pursuing a non-traditional career path.

We will also explore the different techniques that can be employed to overcome these challenges and turn your dreams into a reality. So, buckle up and get ready to learn the tools and techniques you need to succeed in the world of mental unemployability.

Coming up next, we will go into greater detail about how to identify your genuine interests. Finding your passion can unlock your full potential and help you find your true calling. Stay tuned for the next chapter to explore this exciting and transformative topic.

Chapter 2: Finding Your Passion

Finding your passion is vital when chasing a career or starting a business. Your passion will drive your success, and it will keep you motivated even during the most challenging times. In this chapter, we will pinpoint some proven techniques you can utilize in discovering your passion. Also, we will discuss the challenges of finding your passion and provide remedies to overcome them.

Passion is the fuel that drives us towards success in our careers and business endeavors. It is defined as a solid and intense desire towards something we love and enjoy doing. Finding your passion is essential to achieving success in your professional life, as it helps you stay motivated and focused even during difficult times.

Passion is essential for several reasons. Firstly, it gives us a sense of purpose and fulfilment in our work, making it more enjoyable and satisfying. When we are passionate about what we do, we are more likely to put in the effort and time required to excel in our field, resulting in better performance and increased productivity. Additionally, passion helps us to be more creative and innovative in our approach, as we are constantly driven to find new and better ways of doing things. It can also inspire others and positively impact our communities, making our work more meaningful and fulfilling.

Challenges and Remedies to Finding Your Passion

Many people struggle with identifying what inspires and motivates them to take action. Below are some potential challenges you will likely encounter while trying to identify your passion.

Fear of Failure

One of the biggest challenges in finding your passion is the fear of failure. This fear can paralyses you from exploring new interests and taking risks. However, the remedy for this is simple – embrace failure. Failure is a natural part of the entrepreneurial journey. Don't let it discourage you. Embrace failure as a learning opportunity and use it to refine your passion and your business or career.

Lack of Self-Awareness

Another challenge in finding your passion is the lack of self-awareness. Many people have not taken the time to reflect on their interests, strengths, and weaknesses. The remedy is to engage in self-reflection exercises, such as journaling or meditation. These practices can help you identify what truly makes you happy and fulfilled.

Limited Exposure

Sometimes, people struggle to find their passion because they have limited exposure to different experiences and opportunities. The remedy for this is to seek out new adventures, whether attending workshops, travelling to new places, or volunteering for a cause. These experiences can help you discover new interests and passions.

Pressure from External Sources

Finally, another challenge in finding your passion is pressure from external sources, such as family, friends, or societal expectations. The remedy is blocking out the noise and focusing on what makes you happy. Remember, your life and your happiness are your responsibility.

How To Identify What You Are Truly Passionate About

Here are some tips and techniques to help you identify your true passion and turn it into a successful business or a profitable career.

Take a break

Sometimes, the pressure to find your passion can be overwhelming. Take a break and give yourself time to explore new hobbies and interests. This can help you discover new passions that you never knew existed. You could be working as a software engineer, and you've been feeling unfulfilled in your job for a while. Instead of jumping straight into a new career path, take some time to explore new hobbies and interests that catches your curiosity. You may find that you have a talent for photography or a love for pottery that you never knew existed.

What Are Those Things You Love?

The essential step to finding your passion is to think about what you love to do. Understanding what you value most in life is a massive and crucial step to finding your passion. What are your hobbies, interests, and favorite activities? Consider these things and try to identify patterns or themes.

You may always be reading and learning about new topics and love writing in your free time. This could point to a journalism, publishing, or content creation career. Do you love cooking and experimenting with new recipes? You could explore a career in the culinary arts, catering, or food blogging. Are you always organizing events and bringing people together? Maybe you have a knack for event planning or community organizing.

Be Open to New Ideas

Sometimes, our passions and skills can lead us in unexpected directions. Be open to exploring new ideas and opportunities, even if they don't fit neatly into your initial plan. Imagine you've always wanted to be a graphic designer and have spent years honing your skills. However, one day, you stumble upon a coding tutorial and realize you have a programming knack. Even though it wasn't part of your original plan, you explore this newfound interest and eventually create your website.

Try New Things

Don't be afraid to try new things. Attend workshops, take classes, and try out new hobbies. This can help you discover new passions and skills that can be used in your business. If you want to start a consulting business, attend a workshop on public speaking to improve your communication skills and gain confidence when presenting to clients.

Attend a culinary class to learn new dishes and methods you can use in your home if you want to start a food-related company. Take a course in audio production if you create a podcast; it will help you tremendously with the final recordings.

Consider Your Lifestyle

Starting a career or a business can be all-consuming, so it's essential to consider your lifestyle when choosing your passion. Will your business allow you to maintain a work-life balance that aligns with your values and priorities? If you value spending time with your family, consider choosing a career or starting a business that allows you to work from home or have flexible hours. Start a company that requires you to travel for work or that you can run from anywhere if that is something you appreciate doing.

Evaluating Your Skills Finding Your Niche in The Market

Once you've identified your interests, think about your skills and learn how to evaluate them. The process of evaluation will require you to ask questions. What are you good at? What are your strengths and weaknesses? Knowing your skills can help you identify the areas where you can excel in your new career or business.

Let's say you're interested in starting a tutoring business. You can identify your skills by asking yourself, "Am I knowledgeable in a particular subject or multiple subjects?" "Can I effectively communicate concepts and ideas to students?" "Do I have experience managing a schedule or coordinating with parents?" Knowing your skills can help you focus on your abilities, such as a theme, age group, or resource management.

Finding a niche in the market that aligns with your passion and skills is essential. Look for a gap in the market that aligns with your passions and skills. Find a problem that needs solving or isn't being met, and start a career or create a business that addresses that need. This will help you stand out from your competitors.

Maybe you're passionate about fitness and have skills in marketing. You could look for a gap in the market by identifying a need for fitness programs that cater specifically to seniors. Many gyms and fitness studios focus on younger demographics, leaving seniors feeling left out. You could start a fitness program that caters to seniors, using your marketing skills to spread the word and attract clients.

Moving Forward

Finding your passion is a journey that requires self-reflection, exploration, and a willingness to embrace failure. Overcoming potential challenges and learning to identify your passion will help you discover what inspires you and motivates you to take action. Properly evaluating your skills and learning how to find your niche in the market will also position you for greater chances of success in your chosen career or business."

As you continue on your journey to becoming mentally unemployable, you may feel overwhelmed by the number of potential business ideas and directions you could take. But fear not because in the next chapter, you will learn how to harness the power of brainstorming to bring your ideas to life.

Get ready to unlock your creativity and discover innovative ways to turn your passions into a profitable business. The possibilities are endless, and the next chapter will inspire and motivate you to take your ideas to the next level. Get ready for a brainstorming adventure like no other!

Chapter 3: Brainstorming Your Ideas

Brainstorming is a crucial part of the entrepreneurial process. It's a way to explore and generate new ideas that have the potential to turn into successful businesses. But how do you go about brainstorming your ideas? And how do you evaluate them to determine if they are feasible? This chapter will discuss some practical tips and techniques to help you generate and evaluate your ideas effectively.

Firstly, it's essential to know that brainstorming is not just about sitting down and coming up with ideas. It's a process that requires a lot of preparation and research. Start by researching the market, industry, and potential competitors. This will help you identify gaps in the market that you can fill with your business idea. Once you have a better understanding of the market, it's time to start brainstorming.

How To Use Brainstorming Techniques

Brainstorming techniques can be a powerful tool to help individuals who have recently discovered their passion for a career or starting a business. Once you have identified your area of interest, engaging in brainstorming sessions to explore potential ideas and opportunities can be beneficial. Brainstorming is a creative problem-solving process that encourages free thinking and idea generation and encourages you to build upon your ideas.

There are several brainstorming techniques that you can employ to explore different avenues and generate new ideas. For example, you can use the traditional method of listing all potential ideas on a piece of paper, or you can use mind mapping to organize your thoughts visually. Another technique is called "reverse brainstorming," where you explore the opposite of your goal, identifying potential obstacles or challenges that could arise.

Brainstorming techniques are effective for generating ideas and can help you narrow down and focus on the most promising ones. By analyzing and evaluating each concept based on its feasibility, potential impact, and alignment with your values and goals, you can select the best options to pursue.

The Traditional Method

The traditional method of brainstorming involves gathering a group of people and having a free-flowing discussion where everyone can contribute their thoughts and ideas.

One way to make this method more effective is by setting a clear objective and guidelines for the brainstorming session. For example, if you're starting a business in the fashion industry, you could aim to develop five unique marketing strategies targeting a specific demographic. This will help keep the conversation focused and prevent it from going off-topic.

Another tip is to encourage everyone to share their ideas, no matter how wild or unconventional they may seem. Sometimes, the most creative solutions come from thinking outside the box. For example, if you're brainstorming ideas for a new restaurant, someone might suggest having a mobile food truck instead of a traditional brick-and-mortar location. While this idea may seem unconventional initially, it could be a game-changer for the business.

Mind Mapping

Mind mapping is a visual brainstorming technique that allows you to explore and connect different ideas in a non-linear way. To create a mind map, start with your main idea or goal and branch out, adding subtopics, related concepts, and connections.

For example, if your passion is baking and you want to start a bakery, your main idea might be "Opening a Bakery." From there, you can branch out with subtopics like "Types of baked goods to sell," "Location options," and "Marketing strategies." Adding more branches and ideas allows you to see how they relate and form a cohesive plan. Mind mapping can be done on paper or using digital tools. Give it a try and see where your ideas take you!

Reverse Brainstorming

This technique flips traditional brainstorming, focusing on identifying obstacles and roadblocks instead of potential solutions. Doing so helps you anticipate and avoid potential problems, making your passion project more successful in the long run.

For example, imagine you're passionate about opening a new café in town. You could use reverse brainstorming to identify potential obstacles to your success, such as a lack of foot traffic in your desired location, high rent costs, or difficulty finding quality staff. Once you have these potential obstacles identified, you can start coming up with creative solutions to overcome them. Perhaps you could offer a loyalty program to attract customers or negotiate a lower rent cost with your landlord.

Another example could be someone passionate about starting a career in graphic design. Using reverse brainstorming, they could identify obstacles like limited job opportunities, high competition, and limited resources for learning new design software. Armed with this knowledge, they could start looking for ways to stand out in the industry, such as creating a unique personal brand or taking advantage of free online resources to learn new design skills.

How To Evaluate Your Ideas and Determine If Your Idea Is Feasible

Once you have a list of potential ideas, it's time to evaluate them. Start by assessing the feasibility of each idea. Is there a need for the product or service you are proposing? Can you create it within your budget? Is it something you are passionate about? These are all critical questions to ask yourself. Additionally, it's essential to consider the competition. Is there already an established market for your product or service, and if so, how can you differentiate yourself from the competition?

After assessing the feasibility of your ideas, it's time to refine them. Consider the strengths and weaknesses of each idea and how you can build upon them. Be creative and think outside the box. Try to come up with a unique selling point for your business idea. What makes it different from anything else on the market?

When you have narrowed down your list of potential ideas, doing some market research is essential. Look at similar products or services and how they are marketed and priced. Talk to potential customers and get feedback on your ideas. This will help refine your business concept and make it more appealing to your target market.

It's important to note that not all ideas will be feasible or viable. Letting go of an idea and moving on to the next one is okay. Don't get discouraged if your first few ideas don't work out. Keep brainstorming and refining until you find a statement that you are genuinely passionate about and that has the potential to be successful.

Another critical consideration when brainstorming is to think about the future of your business. How scalable is your idea? Will it grow and evolve with the market? It's essential to have a long-term vision for your business and to consider how it will fit into the broader industry landscape.

In addition to brainstorming techniques, having a supportive network of people is crucial. This can be friends, family, or other entrepreneurs. They can offer valuable feedback and insights that can help you refine your ideas and make them more viable.

Lastly, don't be afraid to pivot or change course if needed. As you progress with your business, you may encounter new challenges and opportunities that require you to pivot your strategy. Be flexible and willing to adapt to changing circumstances.

But coming up with a viable business idea is only the first step in the entrepreneurial journey. The real challenge lies in bringing that idea to life and making it profitable. And to do that, you need to know your market inside and out.

You need to understand your customers, your competition, and industry trends. The next chapter in this journey is so crucial: researching the market. It's where the real work begins, where you'll dive deep into data and analytics, and where you'll start to see your idea take shape in the real world. So, brace up because the journey is still ahead, and the pathway is full of challenges and opportunities.

Chapter 4: Researching the Market

Consider this as one of the critical steps. The importance of gathering relevant data and conducting a thorough market and competition analysis cannot be overemphasized. Also, ensuring a viable demand for your product or service is essential before investing time, effort, and resources. This process will help you make informed decisions and increase the likelihood of success. In this regard, it's essential to clearly understand your target audience, their needs and preferences, and the current trends in your industry.

How To Gather Data

To start a successful business or launch your dream career, you need to know your market inside and out. Gathering data is the first step in researching your market, and it's essential to do it right.

This can be done through online research, surveys, or focus groups. Look for trends in the market, and identify gaps that you can fill with your business idea. Don't limit yourself to just one source of information - the more data you have, the better.

Don't Rely Solely on Google Searches

While Google can provide helpful information, it's not the only data source. For example, consider conducting surveys or focus groups with your target audience to gather more specific information about their needs and preferences. This can provide valuable insights that may not be readily available through online research alone.

You could also look into industry reports and studies from reputable sources, such as trade associations or government agencies. These can provide a more comprehensive and unbiased market view than individual websites or articles. The key to effective market research is to use various sources and methods to gather as much information as possible. By doing so, you can better understand your target audience and make more informed decisions about your business or career.

Use Social Media To Gather Data

Monitor conversations related to your market and look for patterns and trends. Attend industry events and conferences. This can allow you to meet potential customers and competitors and learn about the latest industry trends. For instance, if you plan to launch a food delivery service, you can use social media listening tools to monitor conversations related to food delivery, meal prep, and food trends. By analyzing these conversations, you can identify patterns and trends to help you make informed decisions about your business.

Attending Industry Events and Conferences

Utilize your network. Talk to people you know who work in your industry or who have experience starting a business. They may have valuable insights and connections. For example, if you plan to create an e-commerce store, attending industry events such as e-commerce conferences can help you learn about the latest e-commerce trends, network with industry experts, and gain valuable insights into your market. You can also attend seminars, workshops, and panel discussions to gain a deeper understanding of the challenges and opportunities in your market.

Utilizing Market-Related Keywords

This can help you optimize your website and content for search engines. Keyword research involves identifying the words and phrases people use when searching for information related to your market. Using tools such as Google Keyword Planner or SEMrush, you can generate a list of relevant keywords and phrases.

For a fashion e-commerce store, some standard search terms related to your market could be "trendy outfits," "affordable clothing," "summer fashion trends," or "stylish accessories." Including these keywords in your product descriptions and blog posts can improve your chances of appearing in search results.

Once you have a list of relevant keywords, you can use them to optimize your website and content for search engines. This means incorporating the keywords into your website's title tags, meta descriptions, and content to improve your search engine rankings and attract more organic traffic.

How To Analyze the Competition

Once you've gathered your data, it's time to analyze your competition. You need to know who your competitors are, what they offer, and how they operate. Start by doing a Google search for businesses in your industry. Look at their websites, social media pages, and reviews to understand what they do well and where they fall short. Don't forget to look at local businesses too. Visit their stores, interact with their staff, and try their products or services. This will give you a firsthand experience of what they offer and how they operate.

Look at how they're marketing themselves and their strengths and weaknesses. Once you've identified your competitors, create a spreadsheet to keep track of their strengths, weaknesses, and unique selling propositions (USPs). Use this information to identify gaps in the market and opportunities for your business. This will help set you apart from your competition.

Let's consider this example. Suppose you are starting a new restaurant business in your town. After gathering your data about the food industry, you decide to analyze your competition. You begin by collecting data about restaurants in your area. You find that several other restaurants offer a similar cuisine to yours. You then visit their websites and social media pages to learn more about their menus, prices, and ambience. You also read their customer reviews to see what customers like and dislike about their experience. After researching, you identify areas where your restaurant can differentiate itself, such as by offering more unique dishes or creating a more welcoming atmosphere.

But don't stop at analyzing your competition; look at potential partners and collaborators. Who can you work with to make your idea even better? Who can you learn from?

Determine If There Is a Demand for Your Product or Service

Now that you understand the market and your competition, it's time to determine if there is a demand for your product or service. Look at existing data, such as search engine trends and social media buzz. Talk to potential customers and get their feedback on your idea. And don't forget to test your idea on a small scale before committing to a full launch.

Suppose you're launching a new line of vegan protein bars. Before committing to a full launch, you should test your product on a small scale. You could create a limited number of protein bars and distribute them at a local gym or health food store. This would allow you to get feedback from real customers and make any necessary adjustments before launching on a larger scale.

One important thing to keep in mind throughout this process is to stay true to your vision. Don't let the competition or market trends sway you from your original idea. Instead, use this information to refine and strengthen your idea. Another thing to remember is that failure is a natural part of the process. Not every idea will be successful, and that's okay. Use your failures as opportunities to learn and grow, and don't give up. And remember, starting a business is a journey, not a destination. There will be ups and downs, but staying focused and committed to your vision can create something remarkable.

So, take the time to research the market, analyze your competition, and determine if there is a demand for your product or service. Use this information to refine and strengthen your idea, and don't forget to stay true to your vision. You can turn your idea into a successful business with hard work and determination. As you go further, you'll quickly discover that having a solid business plan is the key to success. The next chapter will guide you through creating a comprehensive program covering all business aspects.

Chapter 5: Writing a Business Plan

Choosing to be an entrepreneur is a huge accomplishment, and if you have made it this far, I hope you will accept my heartfelt congratulations on this milestone. But before you start investing your time and money, writing a business plan is essential.

Now it's time to implement your ideas and turn them into a viable business. In this chapter, we will review the fundamentals of writing a business plan, including how to assemble a sales and marketing strategy, a finance plan, and a management structure.

What Is a Business Plan

A business plan is a roadmap that outlines your business's goals, strategies, and tactics for achieving those goals. It serves as a blueprint for your business and provides a framework for decision-making. Writing a business plan is crucial because it forces you to think through every aspect of your business and consider potential roadblocks and challenges.

Suppose you plan to start a new online retail business selling handcrafted products. You have a passion for art and crafts and believe there is a market for unique and handmade products. Before launching your business, you decide to write a business plan.

Your business plan outlines your business's goals, such as the number of customers you want to attract and the revenue you want to generate in the first year. It also includes your strategies for achieving those goals, such as creating a social media presence, building a website, and partnering with influencers to promote your products.

Your business plan also includes details about your target audience, such as their demographics, interests, and purchasing behaviors. It outlines your products' unique selling points, such as the materials used, the level of customization offered, and the pricing strategy.

Your business plan includes a detailed financial plan, including startup costs, revenue projections, and break-even analysis. You also consider potential challenges and roadblocks, such as competition, supply chain issues, and shipping delays.

Thing To Keep in Mind Before Writing a Business Plan

One important thing to remember when writing your business plan is to keep it simple and concise. Avoid jargon and technical terms that may confuse your audience. Remember, your business plan is a tool to help you communicate your vision to potential investors, partners, and employees.

When creating your business plan, it's essential to be realistic and transparent. Don't overestimate your revenue or underestimate your expenses. Be honest about potential risks and challenges, and develop a mitigation plan.

Finally, be sure to include a section on your growth strategy. This outlines how you plan to scale your business over time. Consider potential expansion opportunities, such as new product lines or geographic markets. Additionally, outline your funding strategy and how you plan to secure funding to support your growth.

Creating A Sales and Marketing Plan

This plan outlines how you plan to reach your target audience and promote your product or service. Start by defining your target audience and understanding their needs and pain points. Then, research your competition to identify gaps in the market and opportunities for differentiation.

Based on this information, develop a marketing strategy, including social media marketing, email marketing, and influencer partnerships. Creating a marketing strategy might look something like this:

- **Social media marketing**: We'll create a strong presence on social media platforms like Instagram and Twitter, where fitness enthusiasts will likely spend time. We'll post engaging content that showcases the app's features and benefits and encourage users to share their own experiences with the app using a branded hashtag.
- **Email marketing**: We'll create an email list of users who have downloaded the app and send regular emails with workout tips, motivational messages, and updates on new features.
- **Influencer partnerships**: We'll identify fitness influencers on social media who align with our brand values and offer them a partnership to promote our app to their followers. This could include providing a free app trial, asking them to create content showcasing their experience with the app, or running a giveaway with their followers.

In a nutshell, your marketing strategy should focus on building a solid online presence, fostering a community of engaged users, and leveraging the power of social media and influencer marketing to reach a wider audience.

Creating A Financial Plan

Another essential part of your business plan is your financial plan. This plan details your business's economic projections, including revenue and expenses, cash flow, and profitability. Here is a step-by-step procedure to create a financial plan for your business:

Identify Your Startup Costs

Your startup costs are your expenses before you launch your business. They can include legal fees, marketing expenses, equipment purchases, and office rent. For example, let's say you're starting a small bakery, and your startup costs include renting a commercial kitchen space for $2,500 per month, purchasing baking equipment for $10,000, and paying for a website and logo design for $5,000. Your total startup costs would be $17,500.

Identify Your Ongoing Expenses

Your ongoing expenses are the costs to keep your business running after you launch. These can include things like rent, salaries, utilities, and inventory. Using our bakery example, let's say your ongoing expenses include the monthly rent of $2,500, salaries for two employees at $3,000, utilities at $500, and ingredients and other supplies at $2,000. Your total ongoing expenses would be $8,000 per month.

Estimate Your Revenue

Your revenue is the money you'll bring from selling your products or services. To estimate your revenue, you'll need to clearly understand your target market, pricing strategy, and sales projections. For example, let's say your bakery will sell cupcakes for $3 each, and you estimate you'll sell 1,000 cupcakes per month. Your monthly revenue would be $3,000.

Calculate Your Profitability

To calculate your profitability, subtract your total ongoing expenses from your monthly revenue. In our bakery example, the monthly revenue is $3,000, and the ongoing total expenditures are $8,000. So the monthly net loss is $5,000. This means the bakery is not profitable yet.

Develop a Contingency Plan

A contingency plan is a backup plan for what you'll do if your revenue falls short of your projections. For example, you could reduce your ongoing expenses by renegotiating your lease, reducing employee salaries, or finding cheaper suppliers for ingredients.

Creating A Management Plan

Your management plan outlines the key personnel in your business and their roles and responsibilities. Additionally, this plan outlines how your organizational structure and how decisions will be made.

- **Define Your Business Goals and Objectives:** Before you can identify and achieve your business goals, you must first define your business goals and objectives. What are you trying to accomplish with your business? What are your short-term and long-term objectives? Understanding your business goals and objectives will help you determine what roles and skills you need on your team.
- **Identify The Key Roles and Responsibilities Needed:** Based on your business goals, identify the key roles and responsibilities needed to achieve those goals. Consider the skills and expertise required for each role and the experience level.

- **Create Job Descriptions and Bios for Each Role:** Create job descriptions for each role and identify the required skills and experience. Also, create bios for each team member and highlight their skills, experience, and contributions to the business's success.
- **Outline Your Organizational Structure:** Outline your organizational structure and how decisions will be made. Identify who reports to whom and who is responsible for making decisions. Also, identify any external partners or vendors that your business relies on.
- **Review And Refine the Management Plan:** Review and refine the plan regularly to ensure it remains relevant and practical. Make adjustments based on changes in the business environment or new business goals.

By creating a comprehensive business plan, you have a roadmap that outlines your goals, strategies, and tactics for achieving success. You can use your business plan to make informed decisions, measure progress, and pivot when necessary.

As you finalize your business plan, you can't help but feel a sense of excitement and anticipation for what's to come. Your goals are set, strategies are in place, and you're ready to run. But as you turn the page to the next chapter, "Financing Your Business," a twinge of anxiety creeps in. How will you fund this venture? Will investors be interested in your idea? Can you secure a loan without a proven track record? The next chapter holds the key to unlocking your financial resources to realize your dream.

Chapter 6: Financing Your Business

As you dive deeper into starting your own business, one question looms: how will you finance your venture? It's a question that can strike fear into the hearts of even the most intrepid entrepreneurs. But fear not, my fellow "mentally unemployable" compatriots, for I am here to guide you through financing your business.

Tips On How to Finance Your Business

You can pursue a few different types of financing, depending on your needs and circumstances. One option is to seek a loan from a bank or other financial institution. This can be a good choice if you have a solid credit history and collateral to offer. However, remember that loans come with interest rates and fees, so factor these into your budget.

Another option is to look for grants or other funding opportunities. This can be more competitive, but it's worth exploring if you meet the eligibility requirements. There are many organizations out there that offer grants to small businesses, particularly those in underserved communities or industries.

A third option is to try crowdfunding, which involves raising money from many people via online platforms like Kickstarter or GoFundMe. Crowdfunding can be a great way to build buzz around your business and get early adopters on board, but it can also be time-consuming and require a lot of marketing effort.

No matter which financing option you choose, it's essential to have a solid business plan in place. This will help you demonstrate to lenders or investors that you have a clear vision for your business and a method for achieving your goals.

When seeking financing, it's also essential to be prepared to negotiate. This can mean negotiating the terms of a loan or investment or negotiating with potential partners or vendors to get the best possible deals. Don't be afraid to advocate for yourself and your business – after all, you're the one who knows it best.

How To Create a Budget

The first step in financing your business is to create a budget. This might sound daunting, but trust me; it's easier than you think. Start by listing all the expenses you anticipate in the first year of your business. This might include rent, utilities, inventory, marketing, and employee salaries. Be as detailed as possible in your budgeting, and don't forget to account for unexpected expenses.

Determine Your Fixed Costs

Fixed costs are the expenses that remain constant regardless of how much you sell or produce. These can include rent, utilities, insurance, salaries, and taxes. List all your fixed costs, and include every expense, even the small ones. Once you have your list, total the costs to determine your monthly fixed expenses.

Calculate Your Variable Costs

Variable costs fluctuate based on how much you produce or sell. These can include raw materials, marketing costs, and inventory expenses. Determine your variable costs by estimating how much you will sell each month and the associated costs. Once you have your list, total the costs to determine your monthly variable expenses.

Determine Your Breakeven Point

The breakeven point is when your total revenue equals your total costs. Add your fixed and variable expenses together to determine your breakeven point. Divide that number by your expected monthly revenue to determine how many units you need to sell to break even.

How To Manage Your Finances

Once you have a budget, stick to it. This is easier said than done, but it's crucial to the success of your business. Track your expenses and revenue, and make adjustments as needed. If you're consistently overspending, it's time to find ways to cut costs. Here are some steps to consider.

Separate Your Personal and Business Finances

Your business is not your piggy bank. Separate your finances ASAP. Get a separate bank account and a credit card for your business. This will make it easier for you to keep track of your expenses and income. Determine your fixed and variable costs. Fixed expenses include rent, utilities, insurance, and salaries. Variable expenses are those that change, such as marketing and inventory. Set a monthly budget, and stick to it.

Keep Track of Your Cash Flow

Cash is king. Monitor your cash flow regularly. Keep track of your accounts receivable (money owed to you) and accounts payable (money you owe). Ensure you have enough cash to pay and invest in your business.

Find Funding

Unless you have a rich uncle, you'll need to find funding for your business. There are several options: loans, grants, crowdfunding, and investors. Do your research and find the best option for you. Bootstrapping, or using your money to fund your business, is one option. It may require you to save up for a while, but it gives you complete control over your finances and business. Crowdfunding, loans and investors are other options to consider. Each has its pros and cons, so do your research and choose the option that's best for you.

Monitor Your Financial Statements

Don't bury your head in the sand. Review your financial statements regularly. Look at your profit and loss, balance, and cash flow statements. These reports will give you a snapshot of your financial health. It's easy to get caught up in the excitement of success and overspending, but that can lead to trouble. Make a habit of reviewing your budget and financial statements regularly, and make adjustments as needed.

Managing your finances may not be your favorite part of running a business, but it's crucial. Follow these steps, and you'll be on your way to financial success. And who knows, maybe someday you can retire on a private island.

As you see financial success, it's only natural to start thinking about expanding your business. But how can you do it all on your own? That's where building your team comes in. The next chapter will explore the crucial steps you need to take to find the right people, build a strong team, and take your business to the next level. But be warned, not all hires are created equal, and the wrong team member can bring everything down. So, buckle up and get ready to learn the ins and outs of building a team that will take your business to new heights.

Chapter 7: Building Your Team

Let's face it: You can't do it alone. No matter how brilliant you are, having others to help you build your dream would be best. That's why building a solid team is crucial for any entrepreneur, especially those "mentally unemployable" and determined to make it independently. In this chapter, you will learn some tricks for identifying and recruiting top talent. We will talk about how to keep workers happy and engaged, as well as the various tasks that need to be completed by each team member.

But how do you find the right people? How do you know who to hire and who to avoid? And once you have a team, how do you keep them motivated and focused on your goals? Here are some tips to help you build your dream team:

Know What You're Looking For

Before looking for team members, you must know what you're looking for. What skills do you need? What are personality traits important? What values do you want your team members to share?

Network, Network, Network

The best way to find great team members is through your network. Talk to friends, family, and colleagues. Attend networking events and conferences. Join online communities and forums. You never know who might know the perfect person for your team.

Look For Passion, Not Just Experience

When interviewing potential team members, don't just focus on their experience. Look for passion and enthusiasm for your mission. Someone excited about your work will be more motivated and dedicated than someone just looking for a job.

Ask The Right Questions

During the interview, ask the right questions to assess the candidate's fit with your team. Ask about their values, their work style, and their goals. Ask for specific examples of how they've handled challenging situations.

Don't Rush the Hiring Process

It's better to take your time and find the right person than to rush and hire the wrong one. Don't be afraid to have multiple rounds of interviews or to ask candidates to complete a test or project to demonstrate their skills.

Provide A Clear Vision and Goals

Once you have a team, ensure everyone is on the same page. Provide a clear vision for your company and specific goals to work towards. This will help keep everyone motivated and focused.

Communicate Regularly

Communication is vital to any successful team. Make sure you have regular check-ins with your team members to provide feedback, answer questions, and address any concerns they may have.

Encourage Collaboration and Creativity

A great team works well together and is open to new ideas. Encourage collaboration and creativity by holding brainstorming sessions, promoting cross-functional teams, and creating a culture of experimentation.

Offer Competitive Compensation and Benefits

Money isn't everything, but offering competitive compensation and benefits is essential to attract and retain top talent. Research industry standards and provide a fair and competitive package.

Recognize And Reward Success

Finally, recognize and reward your team members for their hard work and successes. This can be through bonuses, promotions, or simply public recognition. When your team feels valued and appreciated, they will be more motivated to continue working towards your shared goals.

The Different Roles and Responsibilities of Each Team Member

A team comprises individuals with various roles and responsibilities that are vital for the smooth running of the business. First, there is the visionary. This person comes up with the overall direction and strategy for the business. They are the dreamers and thinkers who bring big ideas to the table. They are also responsible for ensuring that the team stays focused on the long-term goals.

Second, there is the manager. This person is responsible for the day-to-day operations of the business. They ensure that the team is working efficiently and effectively. They are also responsible for managing the budget and resources and meeting deadlines.

Third, there is the marketing specialist. This person is responsible for promoting the business to potential customers. They create and execute marketing strategies that will attract and retain customers. They are also responsible for measuring the effectiveness of marketing campaigns and making adjustments where necessary.

Fourth, there is the technical specialist. This person is responsible for the technical aspects of the business. They ensure that the technology used in the business is up-to-date and working efficiently. They also troubleshoot any technical issues that arise.

Finally, there is the customer service representative. This person ensures customers are satisfied with the product or service. They answer customer questions, address complaints, and provide support.

How To Motivate and Retain Your Employees

First and foremost, it's essential to recognize that everyone is motivated by different things. Some people are motivated by money, while others are inspired by recognition or a sense of purpose. Please get to know your employees and figure out what makes them tick. Then, use that knowledge to motivate them. For example, if you have an employee who is motivated by recognition, make sure to acknowledge their accomplishments publicly.

Another way to motivate your employees is by setting clear goals and expectations. When employees know what is expected of them, they are more likely to be encouraged to meet those expectations. Communicate your goals and expectations clearly, and provide feedback regularly.

Retention is also crucial. After all, what's the point of spending time and money on training an employee if they're going to leave after a few months? One way to retain employees is by creating a positive work environment. This means being supportive, providing opportunities for growth and development, and treating employees with respect.

Another way to retain employees is by offering competitive compensation and benefits. While money isn't the only motivator, it's undoubtedly essential. Ensure to provide fair and competitive salaries, and consider offering benefits like health insurance, retirement plans, and paid time off.

Finally, don't forget to have fun! Work doesn't have to be all serious all the time. Encourage your employees to have fun and get to know each other outside of work. Plan team-building activities, celebrate accomplishments, and create a positive, enjoyable work environment.

Building a great team takes time and effort, but it's worth it. Motivating and retaining your employees will create a team dedicated to your business's success. Plus, you'll have more time to focus on the things that only you can do. So go ahead, and start building that dream team!

As you finalize the critical members of your dream team, you can't help but wonder how you'll showcase your business to the world. You know you have a product or service that people need, but how will you grab their attention? You must explore the marketing world, researching tactics and strategies to make your business stand out.

Chapter 8: Marketing Your Business

Now that you've taken the plunge and started your own business, it's time to spread the word and get people interested in what you offer. Marketing can be overwhelming, but it doesn't have to be. With the right strategies and mindset, you can effectively market your business and create a brand that people will remember. Learn effective marketing techniques in this chapter. It will cover topics such as brand development, customer identification, and analytics.

Creating a Strong Brand

The first step in marketing your business is to define your brand. Your brand is the personality of your business and how people perceive it. It's essential to clearly understand your target audience, their needs, and how your business can solve their problems. Take some time to create a brand that reflects your values, mission, and vision. This will help you stand out and attract the right customers.

An example is a small business owner who runs a health food store. They want to create a brand that reflects their values of promoting health and wellness while also solving the problem of customers who may not have access to healthy food options in their area.

To do this, they may create a brand emphasizing natural and organic ingredients, focusing on locally sourced produce. They may also make a mission statement highlighting their commitment to helping customers live healthier lives. Creating a brand that reflects its values and mission makes it more likely to attract customers who share those values and are looking for healthy food options.

Tips And Strategies on How to Market Your Business

Social media is one of the most effective ways to market your business. Social media platforms like Facebook, Instagram, and Twitter allow you to reach a large audience and engage with your followers. However, it's essential to use social media strategically. Don't just post for the sake of posting. Instead, create a social media strategy that aligns with your brand and goals. Use high-quality images, videos, and graphics to grab people's attention and make your brand stand out.

Another critical aspect of marketing your business is networking. Attend industry events, conferences, and meetups to connect with like-minded individuals and potential customers. Don't be afraid to introduce yourself and pitch your business. Remember, people buy from people they like and trust. Building relationships is critical to growing your business.

Word-of-mouth marketing is another powerful tool that can help you attract new customers. Encourage satisfied customers to leave reviews on your website or social media pages. Offer incentives for referrals, such as discounts or free products. When people hear about your business from someone they trust, they're more likely to give you a try.

Always Measure the Success of Your Marketing Efforts

Don't forget to track your results and adjust your strategy accordingly. Use analytics tools to measure the success of your marketing campaigns and make changes as needed. Remember, marketing is an ongoing process. You may need to tweak your strategy to keep up with changing trends and customer needs.

For example, suppose a company launches an email marketing campaign to promote a new product. They use an analytics tool to track open, click-through, and conversion rates. After a few weeks, they notice that the available rates are low, indicating that the subject email lines may not engage enough.

Based on this data, the company revised the subject lines to make them more attention-grabbing. They also segment their email list to send targeted messages to specific customer groups. As a result, the open rates and conversion rates improve, and the campaign generates more sales.

However, the company continues to monitor the campaign's performance and makes adjustments as needed, such as changing the timing of the emails or offering a different incentive. By using analytics tools to track the campaign's results and making changes accordingly, the company can optimize their marketing strategy to achieve better outcomes over time.

After all, is said and done, you are about to embark on an exciting new chapter of your adventure. You're eager to dive into the strategies and tactics to help you grow your business, but you know it won't be easy. But you're ready for it all?

Chapter 9: Growing Your Business

It's time to level up! But now it's time to take your business to the next level. Growing your business can be a daunting task, but it's essential if you want to achieve your goals. In this chapter, we will provide practical advice on growing your business, including expanding your product or service line, scaling your business, and increasing your customer base.

In this chapter, we will provide practical advice on growing your business, including expanding your product or service line, scaling your business, and increasing your customer base.

Tips On How to Grow Your Business

Let's get one thing straight: growing your business is not for the faint of heart. It takes time, effort, and a lot of hard work. But if you're mentally unemployable, you already know this. You're not the type of person whose content to work a 9-5 job and collect a paycheck. You want something more, something bigger, and something that you can call your own. So, how do you grow your business and take it to the next level? Here are some practical tips to help you get there.

First and foremost, you need to have a solid business plan. This means knowing your target market, understanding your competition, and having a clear vision of what you want to achieve. Once you have this, you can start looking at expanding your product or service line. One option is to add complementary products or services that your existing customers find attractive. For example, if you sell handmade soaps, you could also start offering natural lotions or bath salts. This allows you to upsell your existing customer base and attract new customers interested in those products.

Another option is expanding your product or service line by creating something new. This can be a risky move, but if you've done your research and know there's a demand for it, it can pay off big time. Apple started making computers, but now they're a smartphone, tablet, and wearable technology leader. Of course, you don't have to be Apple to expand your product line successfully. Start small and test the waters to see what works and what doesn't.

In addition to expanding your product or service line, you can look for ways to grow your customer base. One way to do this is through social media. Create a solid online presence by posting regularly and engaging with your followers. This will help you build a loyal following and attract new customers interested in what you offer. You can also consider running targeted ads on social media to reach a wider audience.

Don't be afraid to ask for help. Growing your business can be overwhelming, and it's okay to admit that you can't do it alone. Consider hiring a virtual assistant or outsourcing specific tasks to free up your time and focus on what you do best. You can also contact other business owners in your industry for advice and support. Building relationships with like-minded entrepreneurs can be invaluable for growing your business.

How To Scale Your Business and Increase Your Customer Base

Your current clientele is paramount, so give them your attention first. Happy customers are the best form of advertising. So, ensure you provide excellent customer service, go the extra mile for them, and ask for feedback. This will keep them coming back and lead to word-of-mouth recommendations.

Next, you need to start expanding your customer base. One way to do this is through marketing. Use social media, email marketing, and other advertising channels to reach potential customers. Make sure your marketing efforts are targeted to your ideal customer demographic. You don't want to waste time and money marketing to people uninterested in your product or service.

Another way to grow your business is by offering more products or services. You don't want to put all your eggs in one basket. Consider what else you could offer to complement your existing product or service. This could be something as simple as adding a new flavour or colour option or something more complex like providing a related service.

To scale your business, consider hiring additional staff. While this can be a significant investment, it can also free up your time to focus on growing your business in other areas. Make sure you hire people who are a good fit for your company culture and have the necessary skills and experience.

Finally, don't forget to measure your success. Keep track of your revenue, customer acquisition costs, and other key performance indicators. This will help you make data-driven decisions about how to continue growing your business.

Chapter 10: Conclusions and Final Thoughts

Congratulations once again! You've made it to the end of "Mentally Unemployable." You've learned the importance of developing an entrepreneurial mindset, even if you don't plan to start your own business. We've discussed how the traditional 9-5 work model is changing and how becoming mentally unemployable can help you thrive in this new economy.

Throughout this book, we've discussed the challenges of entrepreneurship, such as financial uncertainty and the need for self-discipline. But we've also talked about the incredible rewards of being your boss, such as personal fulfilment, financial independence, and the ability to impact the world

 positively.

One key takeaway from "Mentally Unemployable" is this: you can take control of your career and create the life you want. It may not be easy, but it is possible. And with the right mindset and resources, you can succeed on your terms.

Of course, entrepreneurship isn't for everyone. But developing an entrepreneurial mindset can still be incredibly valuable. It can help you think creatively, take risks, and solve problems in your personal and professional life. And in today's rapidly changing world, these skills are more critical than ever.

So, what's next? Whether you're an aspiring entrepreneur or simply looking to develop your entrepreneurial mindset, the most important thing is to take action. Start by identifying your passions and strengths and exploring ways to turn them into a career. Connect with like-minded individuals and seek resources and mentors to help you. And remember, success isn't just about making money – it's about finding fulfilment and positively impacting the world around you.

In conclusion, becoming mentally unemployable isn't just about starting a business – it's about taking control of your career and creating a life of purpose and fulfilment. It's about developing your mindset and skills to succeed in today's rapidly changing world. And most importantly, it's about taking action and pursuing your dreams, big or small. So, what are you waiting for? It's time to become mentally unemployable and start creating your desired life!